POLITICS OF MANDAL, KAMANDAL AND HIJAB

VOLUME 2, ISSUE 2 OF BRILLOPEDIA

BHAVYA SHARMA | ISHA SHARMA AND KHUSHI JAIN

Contents

Contents

Preface

"Start writing, no matter what. The water does not flow until the faucet is turned on".

-Louis L'Amour

Hundreds of students and professors are contributing their work to Brain Booster Articles, we are here to provide ample information about Law and Contemporary issues. Our aim is to provide a platform for today's generation to express their views and ideas on law and contemporary law.

Authors

Bhavya Sharma is a B.A.LL.B. student from Indore Institute of law and doing One-Year Advance Diploma in ADR from NALSAR, Hyderabad. He has been into research and publication from his school time. He is also into debates and MUNs. His current research is concerned about the popular political jargon known as "Mandal Politics". He is a multidisciplinary writer. He is open for feedback and discussions at sharmabhavya027@gmail.com

Isha Sharma is a 4th year student of B.A.LL.B. (H) from Indore Institute of Law, Indore. She has written various research papers, articles and blogs in the field of social science and law. She has keen interest in reading and understanding contemporary issues and their legality.

Khushi Jain is a student of B.A.LL.B. (*hons.*) 3rdyear pursuing studies from Indore Institute of Law. She has great interest in writing articles, essays, research papers, case summaries and blogs. She always works towards enhancing her skills and knowledge of law and legal aspects. She is interested to pursue her further career in the field of criminal litigation.

Publication

This research paper is published in volume 2, issue 2 of Brillopedia

CHAPTER ONE

Abstract

In 1979, for recognising the requirements of socially and educationally other backward classes, Mandal commission was incorporated under the chair of B.P. Mandal which was brought in force in 1993, under the prime-ministership of P.V. Narsimha Rao. However absolute politics that continued to be effective in public domain over advantages and disadvantages of reservation to other backward classes., it's conceivable consequences, concealed political agendas etc. became a political agenda. This took a shape of a popular political jargon known as "*Mandal Politics*".

Contemporarily, as a result of aggressive Hindutva nationalism, Kamandal politics community representing Hindutva politics surfaced.

With two distinct religion on each side, communal violence became a constant in the secular India which was ignited by political parties benefiting from them. This resulted in declaration of Muslim pasmanda. Assumptions were made on secularity of Muslims, OBCs and Dalits. International stress by O.I.C. growing day by day. It is observed that India's semblance of a secular nation is tarnishing in international space and significant shift in Muslim electorate in India is likewise one of its products. Hijab row being recent development in the paradigm, Hindutva's foot crusaders leaves no stones unturned to craft the wearing of the hijab a countrywide concern, coincidence being Uttar Pradesh's election approaching. Thus, communal violence in India is being used to cater the needs of election propagandas.

Keywords: Other Backward Classes(OBCs), BharatiyaJanta Party (BJP), Uttar Pradesh (U.P.), Organisation for Islamic commission (O.I.C)

CHAPTER TWO

Research Methodology

Due to the absence of authentic literature sources, the author has primarily referred to online sources that are available for the purpose of research work on the subject. The research has its orientation towards the governmental portals and the authentic legal websites along with the articles in the blogs of legal experts. The research has begun from exploring the history of Mandal and Kamandal politics in India and has gradually progressed through the change it brought in the national and international political, cultural and social ethos of India. The content available online is in its full capacity can be regarded as authentic and duly recognised in this research paper work. For any reference, the footnotes can be looked into.

CHAPTER THREE

Research question

R1- While the position of law with regards to Mandal (referring to reservation policies) and Kamandal (relating to secularism) is well settled, the author(s) would try to identify the inadequacy and aperture which leads social, political and cultural fracas in India by examining the effect of Mandal and Kamandal Politics.

R2- How is the shrinking political status in reference to the Uttar Pradesh election of 2022 is relevant with the Hijab row?

R3- What are the contemporary issues related to this subject matter?

R4- How does Mandal Kamandal politics act as an antagonist to the secular persona of India in international space?

Hypothesis

1. That the Mandal Kamandal politics has a noteworthy role to play in the weakening of Muslim electorate in India.

2. That due to the Mandal Kamandal politics, India's semblance of a secular nation is tarnishing in international space

CHAPTER FOUR

Introduction

Mandal and Kamandal politicsare a political jargon which has germinated from the political ethos of states especially with caste and religion disparity. However due to the 2022 elections held in Uttar Pradesh, the depiction of electoral politics in India is freshly being examined. Location 'Mandal' derives its meaning from Mandal commission of 1979 appointed by then Prime Minister Morarji Desai with the main objective of recognising the requirements of socially and educationally backward classes for considering the query of reservations of seats and quotas. Kamandal on the other hand works as a metaphor which denotes a water vessel used by ascetics signifying Hindutva politics. It refers to Hindutva politics that surfaced parallelly to Mandal politics as a result of aggressive Hindutva nationalism fostered by BJP, pinnacle of which is considered to be *Ram Janam Bhumi* crusade.

CHAPTER FIVE

History

Morarji Desai, the Prime Minister of India in 1979, constituted a commission under the chairmanship of then Member of Parliament from Madhepura constituency Bihar, Babu Bindheshwari Prasad Mandal. The commission was assigned the duty of categorising socially and educationally backward classes in India. They acknowledged an aggregate of 3743 diverse castes and communities being backward on various fronts. These castes encompassed approximately 52% of the aggregated population of India[1]. In suggestions, the commission projected the notion of providing 27% reservation to these backward castes/classes in public service beside SC and ST.

Conversely for nearly a decade this report lingered neglected in public domain until V.P. Singh was made the Prime Minister of India in the year 1989. With numerous political agendas, he resolved to execute suggestions of the Mandal commission. It was his attempt to secure and dominate votes of backward castes with himself in imminent elections. Nevertheless, his attempt got struggled in bureaucratic courses and never-ending judicial interferences.

Decisively in 1993, under the prime-ministership of P.V. Narsimha Rao, suggestions of Mandal Commission were applied after consent was obtained from the honourable Supreme Court of India in the famous case of Indra Sawhney[2].

- **Mandal Politics**- In the meantime the absolute politics that continued to be effective in public domain over advantages and disadvantages of reservation to other backward classes, it's conceivable economic, political and social consequences, concealed political agendas encompassing the suggestions of Mandal commission etc. is inclusively termed as "*Mandal Politics*". It is the residue of Mandal politics that several backward castes for instance Thakur, Yadav, Kurmi etc. who remained within the political boundaries of significant states such as Uttar Pradesh and Bihar came to limelight of the political model of these territories.

- **Kamandal-** In contrast *Kamandal* represents Hindutva politics that surfaced parallelly to Mandal politics as a result of aggressive Hindutva nationalism fostered by BJP. *Ram Janam Bhumi* crusade that concluded through demolition of Babri masjid and consequent renaissance of BJP in Indian political scenario was the pinnacle of Kamandal politics. For the tenure 1991, BJP revived in the state election with a crucial win and formed a government. It triumphed over 221 seats in the Legislative Assembly of 403 members.

Mandal and Kamandal were two divergent streams in Indian political scenario during 1990s and 2000s chiefly in Bihar and UP. Meanwhile BJP beget both Mandal and Kamandal, seeing that in fresh elections backward castes voted overpoweringly in support of BJP according to the election statistics of 2014 General elections[3].

CHAPTER SIX

Aftermath of Mandal Kamandal politics

The outcome of Mandal and Kamandal politics had its effects not only on the politics of India but also on the socio-cultural ethos of the country in numerous aspects. Some of them are brought up below:

1. **Declaration of the Muslim Pasmanda**: Firstly, a few Muslim backward castes were included in the OBC list which legitimise the declaration of the Muslim Pasmanda (an Indian Muslim communal reform group committed for the liberation of the Dalit Muslims associating to the "Arzal" rank in the caste system amongst Muslim of South Asia.). This novel inferior politics countered the mind of Muslim uniformity. Pasmanda probed this caste-based communal division amongst Muslims and claimed that Muslim Dalits should necessarily be incorporated in the SC category.
2. **Muslims Became political community**: Secondly, with the existence of Muslims as a religious minority in the social justice framework played a different role. To reverse BJP's communalism in electoral politics, the non-BJP parties summoned Muslims as a political community to guard secularism. An image was shaped according to which Muslims backed Mandal politics merely to overthrow the BJP's majority rule[1].
3. **No address of the issue**: The non-BJP political parties, nonetheless, persuaded an extremely calculative and conniving tactic concerning Muslim communities. They did not express any significant interest in magnifying the room of social justice framework and persisted to evoke the ancient criticism of Hindu communalism. Though Pasmanda Muslim leaders, such as Ejaz Ali and Ali Anwar Ansari, resolved to become Rajya Sabha Member of Parliament, no political parties, counting the Bahujan

Samaj Party and the Janata Dal (United), openly spoke about the subject of Muslim caste as a social justice question.

4. **Muslims were perceived as the ambassador of secularism**: Their presence was demarcated in a firm orthodox manner. Statistics indicates[2] that the Muslim electorates remained not the lone category that was deployed in opposition to the BJP as a political constituency between the periods of 1996 to 2009. Mandal politics was capable of generating a successful outline of Dalits, OBCs and Muslims contrary to the BJP's superior caste, Hindu electorate. The triumph of non-BJP parties was inseparably connected to this broader anti-BJP. Yet, the mass media driven political debate constantly designated effective Muslim involvement as one of the explanations of the political misfortunes of the BJP, particularly in the 2000s.
5. **No significant agenda for socialmodification**: Mandal politics not yet had any significant agenda for social modification. Political-electoral harmony of the backward classes was foreseen as a tactic to have a comprehensive society. There was no space for social development or societal contact among diverse ignored groups in this frame. As a consequence, an essentialist, exceedingly competitive pressure-group-kind politics instigated to weaken the delicate harmony of the backward communities.
6. **Assumptions on secularity of OBCs and Dalits**: There was a sharp notion that Dalits and OBCS would obviously be secular. The BJP was staged as a political party of higher-class Hindu *manuvadis*, having the aim of creating a religious State — the Hindu *rashtra*. This attitude of perception was anti-productive. The BJP redeveloped its political grounds in an essential way, specifically after the establishment of the National Democratic Alliance (NDA). The party offered a fresh predominant Hindu model to adjust various classes and castes to foster its cautiously build anti-Muslim electoral tactic.

CHAPTER SEVEN

Possible effects of Mandal & Kamandal on Muslims Electoral Politics

- **Pre-Independence Factors-** On August 15, 1947, India gained independence: a moment of birth that was also an abortion, because freedom came with the horror of division, when the leaving British ripped East and West Pakistan from India's bent shoulders[1]. Since the time of pre-independence, most elections in India's Muslim-majority provinces saw the All-India-Muslim-League (AIML) perform poorly. In undivided India, Bengal and Punjab had the highest Muslim populations. Though the AIML had made significant gains in Bengal by the 1940s, the party had been defeated in Punjab in the 1930s elections. The British colonial authority in India called for national and legislative assembly elections in 1945. The Punjab election was scheduled for February 1946. The Congress' goal was to gain a majority in most provinces so that it could advance its claim to build a united (post-colonial) India government. The AIML's purpose was to win elections in Muslim-dominated provinces so that it could claim not only to be the largest Muslim party, but also to assert its desire for a separate Muslim nation-state in places where Muslims were in the majority[2].

- **Post-Independence Factors-** India was divided on the basis of religion. Newly created Pakistan declared 'Republic of Islam' whereas India intent to choose a democratic country. Communities that had coexisted for over a millennium across the Indian subcontinent attacked one another in a terrible outbreak of sectarian warfare, with Hindus and Sikhs on one side and Muslims on the other, in an unexpected and unprecedented mutual extermination. Massacres, burning, forced conversions, mass abductions, and severe sexual abuse were particularly common in Punjab and Bengal, provinces flanking India's borders with West and East Pakistan, respectively. Seventy-five thousand women were raped, with many of them scarred or maimed as a result[3].

- **The Politics begins with-**

Mandal- The religious war did not end with the partition, for a say India is Democratic but the Muslims felt disenchanted. The Union government's decision to offer 4.5 percent reservation among minorities for the Socially and Educationally Backward Classes (B.C.s) within the 27 percent quota for Backward Classes is based on misunderstanding and ignorance[4].

The criticism made for the decisions as follow:

- That the quota is religion based, thus unconstitutional and minorities such as Muslims are not included.
- Reservations for Backward class amidst Muslims is wrong, as Muslims do not recognise caste system.
- It is deemed that reservation is only given to Hindu's Backward class only.
- It assumes, what has been offered currently is either too much or too little for Muslims.

Kamandal-BJP is now banking on Kamandal to overcome the Mandal challenge. All the statements made in the U.P. elections campaigns of 2022 by Yogi Adityanath and Amit Shah are connected with Hindutva and Nationalism. The statements were also made on the issues of Article 370, special status of J&K and even on the Ram Janam Bhoomi. The chief minister Yogi also indicated the election to be a struggle between 80 percent (Hindus) and 20 percent (non-Hindus) (Muslims)[5]. The Kamandal issue started in the 90s, the demolition of the Babri Masjid and the controversies surrounding the Mandal Commission recommendations were among the ups and downs during that time. But we can see the results these days also. The hate between people already started, mainly the increasing disputes between Hindu Muslim.

- **Other communal violence responsible for the religious aggression-**

- In 1969 the Gujarat Communal Riot, 660 people killed[6]
- In 1990 Exodus of Kashmiri Hindus, 300 people killed and 3-5 lakh have migrated[7]
- During 2000 to 2004, North-East India militancy, banned all Hindu celebrations[8].
- Other Anti-Hindu violence- 1998 Chambal massacre, 2002 Attack on Raghunath temple, 2002 Akshardham Temple attack, 2006 Varanasi Bombing, Godara train Attack, etc

- **2014 -The Historic win-** In 2014, Modi's Bhartiya Janata Party's historic election triumph changed the political landscape of the world's largest democracy. "*This is something that Jawaharlal Nehru had predicted,*" Mr. Mukherjee said, referring to India's first prime minister. "*He said if fascism ever came to India it would come in the form of majoritarian Hindu communalism. That is exactly what is happening.*" Around 100 million first-time voters cast ballots in the elections. One of the primary reasons for the BJP's victory looks to be Hindu support. People's Ideology changes, but the arguments of anti-Hindu believes that the India's is leading towards nasty anti-Muslim campaign, but author believe that this Hindutva politics is harming Hindus and that they must resist it because it is in their best interests. It is transforming Hindu youth into enraged mobs and diverting their attention away from the pressing issues that they should be worried about. The government should strive for a balanced acceptance of India's diverse religious communities, without favouring any one group over another.

- **The Haemorrhage effects on the country-** The terms freedom and democracy are frequently used interchangeably, but they are not interchangeable. It is safe to assume that democracy is the institutionalisation of freedom, and the constitution is the bastion of democracy[9]. Thus, Indian Hindus choose their democratic rights to vote BJP, that the party will work in their interest, eventually the dispute of Ram Janam Bhoomi was also solved in the favour of Hindu Voters. Out of the above reasons, Muslims choose not to represent in or for BJP. But the author believes that this will not only affect one community but everyone in the country. The government should work secularly in the development of the country and should pay attention to the issues of the Employment, Poverty, Infrastructure, Education, better health care, a growing economy, etc. The Hindutva and Hindu Nation ideology frame has been set up which is going against the betterment of the country.

CHAPTER EIGHT

Contemporary issues in this research- The Hijab Row

The Hijab row debate fermented in Karnataka after Muslim girls were prohibited from wearing Hijabs (a headscarves worn in community places by certain Muslim females) in colleges and schools. The matter pitches up legal interrogations on whether the right to wear a hijab is constitutionally shielded and reading the freedom of religion.

Various opportunist parties intercede in the issue staunchly opposing each other, with few favouring the ban on the Hijab whereas others backing Muslim girls wearing the Hijab. Student oppositions over Hijab Ban erupted into extensive political debates fostering political parties with a novel election issue, while numerous students appealed for an end to the prejudice.

A. The Karnataka High Court declared that wearing a hijab is not an essential practice in Islam and that 'the prescription of school uniforms is a reasonable restriction.
B. Hijab row: Weighs more on UP than Karnataka?
   Unvexed by other noteworthy judgements, for instance the Puttaswamy judgement[1], on the right to privacy, Hindutva's foot crusaders leave no stones unturned to make the wearing of thc hijab a countrywide concern relating right to attire, coincidence being Uttar Pradesh's election approaching. BJP's past statistics of winning election on communal grounds unturned here.
   For prevailing in the election in UP, parties use communalism by not only crushing the OBC-Jat caste establishment but also by blocking the Muslim vote from uniting to form alliance. The Western part of UP comprises of 136 seats throughout 26 districts where the Muslim

population is marginally over 26 per cent[2].
Western UP is extremely important for parties like Bahujan Samaj Party (BSP) and BJP as in 2017 elections, although BJP had obtained 41 per cent votes in UP, the vote share in Western UP stood 44.14 per cent, partially being the result of communal propaganda relating to Hindus fleeing Kairana. In the general elections of 2019, BJP vote count stood at 50 per cent for the entire state of UP and 52 per cent in Western UP[3].

However, the BJP did not fill any Muslim contender in the area, for the 2022 elections, the SP has stood with 12 Muslim candidates, the Bahujan Samaj Party (BSP) with 16, the Congress with 11, and the All India Majlis-e-IttehadulMusalmeen (AIMIM) with 9[4]. Thus, understanding the popularity of hijab row in the midst of UP elections festivity as a coincidence would be ignorance.

CHAPTER NINE

Commitments made at the international level

India is a diverse country in terms of religion, ethnicity, and language. It is estimated that 200 million Muslims, the majority of which is identified as Sunni, make up to around 15% of the population, making them the country's largest minority group. Hindus account for roughly 80% of the population[1]. While the global population is forecast to rise by 32% over the next few decades, Muslims are expected to grow by 70%, from 1.8 billion in 2015 to over 3 billion in 2060[2].

- **Position in China**- But China has a different position in reference to the Muslims population. In the north-western province of Xinjiang, China has been accused of perpetrating crimes against humanity and potentially genocide against the Uyghur population and other primarily Muslim ethnic groups. Human rights organisations claim China has arrested over one million Uyghurs against their will in a vast network of "re-education centres" and sentenced hundreds of thousands to prison terms in recent years[3].
  According to research on Chinese oppression of Muslim minority, thousands of mosques in Xinjiang have been damaged or demolished in just three years, leaving fewer in the province than at any time since the Cultural Revolution[4].
- **Nehru-Liaquat Samjhota**- After the partition of India-Pakistan, on 8th April 1950 a Pact was signed between India and Pakistan 'Nehru-Liaquat-Agreement.'
  In this "*The government of India-Pakistan solemnly agree that each shall ensure, to the Minorities throughout its territories, complete equality of citizenship, irrespective of their religion, a full sense of security in respect*

of life, culture, property and personal honour, freedom of movement within each country and freedom of occupation, speech and worship, subject to law and morality[5]."

Such steps were taken to ensure the rights of minorities in both nations as communal tensions were at their peak, but no change has been made till the dates.

- **International comments-**
- This internal politics has now become an international problem, the problem of any country should be solved within the country. Shashi Tharoor tweeted a tweet claiming that Kuwaiti legislators have written to India's government urging an immediate ban on BJP members entering the country. This was written "We can't sit back and watch Muslim girls being publicly persecuted."
- Also, the USCIRF noted that religious freedom conditions in India had 'significantly worsened' in 2021, and suggested that India be categorised as a 'Country of Particular Concern,' i.e., the category of government that performs the worst on religious freedom criteria for the third year in a row[6].
- The 57-member OIC, which regards itself as the Muslim world's collective voice, also criticised India for its comments about the Prophet and urged the UN to take action to address "practises targeting Muslims in India"[7].

Year 2012- There were six civil wars in the world in 2012. Afghanistan, Pakistan, Sudan, Somalia, Syria, and Yemen are all Muslim countries where these events occurred. Seven of the nine rebel organisations involved in these clashes were Islamist

CHAPTER TEN

Conclusion

While the position of law with regards to Mandal (referring to reservation policies) and Kamandal (relating to secularism) is well settled, the lacuna is abuse of the diversity that India embraces by the political parties. The practise of divide and rule policy by political parties can be traced back to pre- and post-independence era, climax being execution of suggestions made by the Mandal commission by the then prime minister V.P. Singh with numerous political agendas in 1989.This sowed the seeds of Mandal Kamandal politics, backed by aggressive Hindutva nationalism fostered by BJP. Consequences of this being social, political and cultural fracas in India.

States like U.P. and Bihar suffered utmost damages from this social evil, outcome of which can significantly be seen on decreasing of Muslim electorate in these states. Recent demonstration of the concern being Hijab row, where Hindutva's foot crusaders leave no stones unturned to craft the wearing of the hijab a countrywide concern, coincidence being Uttar Pradesh's election approaching. BJP's past statistics of winning election on communal grounds unturned here. For prevailing in the election in UP, parties use communalism by not only crushing the OBC-Jat caste establishment but also by blocking the Muslim vote from uniting to form alliance. The Western part of UP comprises of 136 seats throughout 26 districts where the Muslim population is marginally over 26 per cent.

Consequences of the aforementioned can be seen international aspect. It is no astonishment that Mandal Kamandal politics act as an antagonist to the secular persona of India in international space. The USCIRF noted that religious freedom conditions in India had 'significantly worsened' in 2021, and suggested that India will be categorised as a 'Country of Particular Concern,' which determines the category of government that performs the worst on religious freedom criteria for the third year in a row.

To combat this issue, the author(s) believe that the government should work secularly in the development of the country and should pay attention to the issues of the Employment, Poverty, Infrastructure, Education, better health care, a growing economy, etc. The Hindutva and Hindu Nation ideology frame has been set up which is going against the betterment of the country.

Printed by Libri Plureos GmbH in Hamburg,
Germany